CHAPTER 1

Define Your F6 Goals and People Who Kill Your Soul

"78 percent of the men interviewed had cheated on their current partner." - *5 Myths About Cheating*

https://www.washingtonpost.com/opinions/five-myths-about-cheating/2012/02/08/gIQANGdaBR_story.html?noredirect=on&utm_term=.05ab54a87466

I've often heard it said that it's lonely at the top. I however passionately disagree. I love life at the top. I love the peacefulness of being only in the company of people that are drama free, and you would like it too. Imagine just for a moment that you had earned all of the money you need and thus you found yourself with an abundance of free time. What would you do

$ = TIME FREEDOM

with all your hardearned free time? ~~who would~~ would you choose to spend your time with? What places would you go and visit? However, imagine for a moment that you were at the perfect place on that perfect beach eating your favorite food while listening to your FAVORITE MUSIC, yet being surrounded by jealous jerks and negative nancys...

Jackassery = wealth repelling beliefs

My friend ~~whenever~~ whenever you are around dramatic, chronically dysfunctional and negative humans the entire joy and happiness of the moment is clouded and ~~ruined~~ crowded out by their jackassery. I remember when my Dad was dying from Lou Gherig's disease and an event was organized in his honor. The food was good, the sentiments were appreciated, but the

~~assholes, maggots,~~ jerks, ~~betraying bastards, backstabbers, negligent idiots,~~ bad people who attended his event made it nearly impossible for me to enjoy. However, on a daily basis I do not experience these ~~was~~ situations ~~on a~~ because I simply refuse to hang out with people who:
* Constantly email full-page drama
* Are late to everything
* ARe Lazy
* constantly have drama in their lives

- irritate me
- want to focus on divisive religious debates
- have affairs consistently
- complain about their spouse
- are aggressively wrong
- are socialists
- consistently don't do what they ~~sa what~~ say
- argue on social media all-day
- want to get rich quick
- are ruled by their emotions
- complain about daylight savings time as though it were going to kill us
- like Bernie Sanders

In order for you and I to achieve happiness we must invest the time needed to define our Goals for the next 12 MONTHS in the areas of:

FAITH: _____
FAMILY: _____
FINANCE: _____
FRIENDSHIP: _____
FITNESS: _____
FUN: _____

You must say "NO" to "Grow".

Now the moment to start setting goals, you must be ready for the tough decisions to be made. You are already filling up your schedule, so what are you going to have to say no to?

- [ ] TV
- [ ] NEGATIVE PEOPLE
- [ ] SOCIAL MEDIA
- [ ] NON-ACTIONABLE NEWS
- [ ] OBLIGATORY FAMILY FUNCTIONS
- [ ] MENTORING COUSINS
- [ ] NETWORKING LUNCHEONS

You must say "No" to "Grow."

- [ ] Talking about being burnt out
- [ ] Talking about your anxiety
- [ ] Getting your eyelashes extended
- [ ] Getting your nails done
- [ ] Watching Netflix
- [ ] Getting massages
- [ ] Traveling and vacationing
- [ ] Starting, but never finishing things
- [ ] Over-volunteering

10

You must say "No" to "Grow."

- [ ] Watching endless YouTube videos on how to get-rich-quick
- [ ] Attending seminars yet never implementing what you are learning
- [ ] Google searching

It is vitally important you decide what ~~too~~ things you will, for a season, say no to in order to grow.

NOW THAT WE HAVE SAID NO TO CERTAIN THINGS OR ~~ACTIVITIES~~ ACTIVITIES, IT'S VITALLY IMPORTANT THAT ~~YOURS~~ YOU MAKE A SPECIFIC LIST OF THE PEOPLE YOU WILL SAY NO TO. OH YES, I'M BEING SERIOUS:

PERSON #1: _____

PERSON #2: _____

PERSON #3: _____

PERSON #4: _____

WHO WILL YOU SAY NO TO?

Who should you unfriend on Facebook Right Now?

_____
_____
_____
_____

Who should block on your phone? _____

Who do you need to push out of your life Right Now? _____

NOTABLE QUOTABLE:
"WALK WITH THE WISE AND BECOME WISE, FOR A COMPANION OF FOOLS SUFFERS HARM." —PROVERBS 13:20

* FOR YOU CHRISTIAN READERS. THIS VERSE IS TRUE EVEN IF WE ARE TALKING ABOUT YOUR FAMILY. YOU MUST BE INTENTIONAL ABOUT WHO YOU WILL ALLOW TO HAVE ACCESS TO YOU.

14

I don't care how much money you earn you will never be happy when surrounded by negative, nefarious and scheming family members. Trust me... I have tried to prop ~~x~~ up negative, lazy and slacker-family members and ~~ever~~ every time it ~~just~~ just makes them more ~~entitl~~ entitled, jealous and unappreciative.

← This is you at the top of Mt. Success when you are surrounded by negative people.

Notable Quotable:
"Do not be deceived: Bad company ruins good morals."
- 1st Corinthians 15:33

16

→ THIS IS YOU AT THE TOP OF MOUNT SUCCESS WHEN YOU ARE SURROUNDED ONLY BY KIND AND JOYFUL PEOPLE.

NOTABLE QUOTABLE
"SURROUND YOURSELF ONLY WITH PEOPLE WHO ARE going to lift you higher." - Oprah Winfrey

The vast majority of Americans hate their jobs or "seven out of 10 workers" have "checked out" at work or are "actively disengaged" according to a recent Gallup survey. Thus, I would not listen to what the vast majority of people have to say. In fact, 78% of the men surveyed by Washington Post have cheated on their current partner.

Why am I writing this? I'm writing this because the vast majority of Americans are people that are wrong and whose personal drama and issues will inhibit the overall level of your happiness. Be careful about who you spend your time with if you want to have a happy life.

CHAPTER 2

It Takes A Grind and a Mastermind

"You're the average of the five people spend the most time with."
— Jim Rohn (Best-selling author and renowned speaker)

IF YOU WANT TO ACHIEVE SUPER SUCCESS IT IS VERY IMPORTANT THAT YOU BUILD A FRIENDSHIP AND NETWORK BASED and comprised of HIGH CHARACTER AND TOP-PERFORMING ~~IDEN~~ INDIVIDUALS. AS AN EXAMPLE, IF I WANTED TO DO THE FOLLOWING THINGS TODAY, I COULD BECAUSE OF THE ~~xxxxx~~ PEOPLE I KNOW.

① Get a $100,000 BANK LOAN

② INTERVIEW AN NFL PLAYER ON THE THRIVETIME SHOW PODCAST

3) INTERVIEW A TOP 40 SONG WRITER ON THE THRIVETIME SHOW PODCAST

4) Get THE ANSWER To ANY BUSINESS QUESTION IMAGINABLE

5) get ANY LEGAL QUESTION ANSWERED

6) TALK WITH THE Highest Elected OFFICIALS IN MY STATE.

7) BUY A CAR 30% OFF MARKET VALUE.

8) ETC.

At the end of the day it will come down to who you know AND WHAT you know IF YOU WANT TO EVER GROW.

~~Doe~~ WHO DO YOU KNOW TODAY IN THE WORLD OF?:

① ACCOUNTING
② BANKING
③ LEGAL
④ ENTREPRENEURSHIP/MENTORSHIP
⑤ REAL ESTATE INVESTING
⑥ FINANCIAL MANAGEMENT

Assuming that you do now have every connection possible, you still must rise and grind or you will be left behind. Today I woke up at 3:00 AM to prepare for my Saturday morning appointments and I have been doing this for nearly 20 consecutive years.

Notable Quotable:
"When you're around enormously successful people you realize their success isn't an accident, it's about work." -Ryan Tedder (Grammy-Award winning song

IT'S VERY IMPORTANT TO SURROUND YOURSELF WITH PEOPLE YOU CAN LEARN FROM.

- Reba McEntire
(American Country Singer, Songwriter, Record Producer, and Actress)

CHAPTER 3

WALK WITH THE WISE AND YOU'LL WIN, WALK WITH IDIOTS AND YOUR WALLET GETS THIN

Following wise owls is a **WONDERFUL** thing...

"Walk with the wise and become wise, for a companion of fools suffers harm." - Proverbs 13:20

It's amazing to me how many business ~~ou~~ owners are placing their incompetent friends, family and ~~acquaint~~ acquaintances in charge simply because they "know" them.

Whether they are your friend or someone you just met you must remember ~~that~~ "Walk with the wise and become wise, for a companion of fools suffers harm." - Proverbs 13:20

Oh, I wish I would have realized that just by being friends with fools I would be harmed.

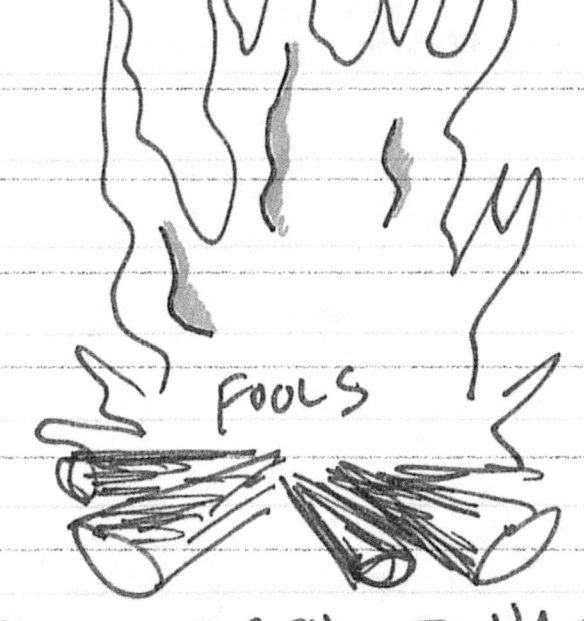

Hence forth, I have committed myself and my time to no longer being around fools.

> "I can't relate to lazy people. We don't speak the same language. I don't understand you. I don't want to understand you."
>
> — Kobe Bryant
> (5-Time NBA Champion, 18-Time NBA All-Star)

CHAPTER 4

THE SECRET TO HAPPINESS

"The secret of happiness is minimizing the amount of time you spend with people you don't choose to be with." – Phil Libin
(Former CEO of Evernote)

WHAT ARE YOU INTENTIONALLY DOING RIGHT NOW TO MINIMIZE YOUR TIME SPENT WITH FOOLS?

- [ ] Defriending people on Facebook.
- [ ] Blocking certain contacts on your phone.
- [ ] Telling certain people that we are "100%" done with each other.

☐ OTHER? _____

WHETHER YOU ARE ~~READY~~ READY TO ACCEPT IT RIGHT NOW OR NOT, THE FORMER CEO OF EVERNOTE HAD IT CORRECT WHEN HE ONCE SAID, "The secret of happiness is minimizing the amount of time you spend with people you don't choose to be with." -PHIL LIBIN (THE FORMER CEO OF EVERNOTE)

32

"A man of many companions may come to ruin, but there is a friend who sticks closer than a brother."

- Proverbs 18:24

CHAPTER 5

Don't Allow Cancerous Relationships to Fester and Grow

"Surround Yourself with Great People. People are what make businesses prosper"
- Wayne Huizenga
(The founder of Autonation, Waste Management, and the creator and initial owner of the Florida Marlins and Panthers)

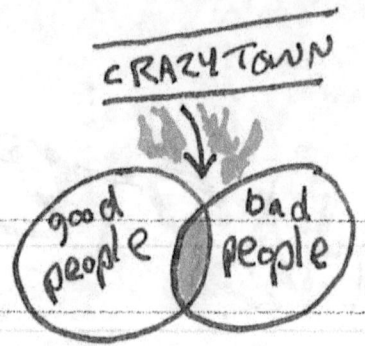

In order to get where we want to go you and I both know that we cannot allow bad relationships to fester and grow. If your partner is cheating on his wife with a member of your customer service team you want to remove that cancerous activity and person from your ~~org~~ organization ASAP (as soon as possible).

If your partner is stealing from your business to buy a massive truck ~~with that your business~~ this is a problem you want to deal with NOW OR AS SOON AS POSSIBLE. IF YOUR PARTNER IS CHRONICALLY LATE TO EVERYTHING YOU NEED TO DEAL WITH THIS AS SOON AS POSSIBLE. If your MANAGERS ARE NOT STARTING THEIR MEETINGS ON TIME YOU WANT TO →

deal with this situation as soon as possible because according to Corinthians 15:33 "Do not be deceived: Bad company ruins good morals." 1st Corinthians 15:33

As for me, I personally cannot handle being around people that choose to be low energy and negative. ⬇ ☹

"Surround yourself with people who take their work seriously, but not themselves, those who work hard and play hard."
  — Retired Four Star General and the 65th United States Secretary of State, Colin Powell)

If you and I are not serious and intentional about dealing with the negative people around us →

Soon we will be forced to change when they break various laws, steal from you, create drama in your life or find a way to steal your happiness by causing you to think about them and their poor life choices even when they are not around. Who in your life is currently cancerous, negative and drama causing?

CHAPTER 6

Don't Lower Your Standards

"Do not be conformed to this world, but be transformed by the renewal of your mind, that by testing you may discern what is the will of God, what is good and acceptable and perfect." - Romans 12:2

You cannot ever lower your standards enough to appease lazy, Godless, and ~~morrs~~ morally relative people. Whether it's insisting that your organization starts everything on time or that your organization only hires A-quality people. Holding your team accountable to a higher standard will require you to make ~~people~~ people mad.

"Be a yardstick. Some people aren't used to an environment where excellence is expected."
— Steve Jobs
(the cofounder of Apple, the former CEO of Pixar and the founder of NeXT)

In what areas have you allowed mediocrity to creep into your life and organization?

_____
_____
_____

"The quality of a person's life is in direct proportion to their commitment to excellence, regardless of their chosen endeavor."
— Vince Lombardi
(The former football coach who lead the Green Bay Packers to five total ~~that~~ NFL championships in 7 years in addition to winning the first two Super Bowls.)

CHAPTER 7

Accept That Most People Are Wrong About Everything All of the Time

FUN FACT - "17 percent of couples are content in their partner." - https://www.psychologytoday.com/us/blog/contemplating-divorce/201709/are-you-among-the-growing-number-unhappy-married-people

FUN FACT - "75% of employees steal from the workplace and most do so repeatedly." - https://www.cbsnews.com/news/employee-theft-are-you-blind-to-it/

FUN FACT - "85 percent of job applicants lie on resumes." - https://www.inc.com/jt-odonnell/staggering-85-of-job-applicants-lying-on-resumes.html

The statistics are not encouraging, but when you take a moment to pause and reflect on them a powerful truth will emerge.

* "83% of couples are not content with their partner." - Psychology Today

* "85% percent of job applicants lie on resumes." - Inc. Magazine

- "75% of employees steal from the workplace and most do so repeatedly."
  – U.S. CHAMBER OF COMMERCE / CBS NEWS

- THUS, I CAN ACCURATELY SAY THAT THE VAST MAJORITY OF PEOPLE ARE WRONG ABOUT:
  * <u>LYING</u>
  * <u>STEALING from the workplace</u>
  * ~~HAVING~~ AFFAIRS / HAVING

In orer for you to achieve success and peace you must stop listening to the advice provided for free by most people most of the time.

Notable Quotable:

"Few people are capable of expressing with ~~equal~~ equanimity opinions which differ from the prejudices of their social environment. Most people are even incapable of forming such opinions." Albert Einstein

CHAPTER 8

GETTING SCHOOLED ON HOW TO DEAL WITH FOOLS

"In the course of your life you will be continually encountering fools. There are simply too many to avoid. We can classify people as fools by the following rubric: when it comes to practical life, what should matter is getting long-term results, and getting the work done in as efficient and creative a manner as possible... You can distinguish them by how little they get done, or by how hard they make it for others to get results. They lack a certain common sense, getting worked up about things that are not really important while ignoring problems that will spell doom in the long term. You can't win an argument or get them to see your side or change their behavior, because rationality and results don't matter to them. You simply waste valuable time and emotional energy." - Robert Greene (Best-Selling author of *Mastery*)

Getting schooled on how to deal with fools is super ~~important~~ important!*

~~We~~ Frankly, we live in a world where fools are all around us and you can ~~get~~ quickly tell who a fool is by asking yourself the following questions about the potentially foolish ~~person~~ person in your life.

1. Does the potential fool actually get alot of real things done?

2. Does the potential fool get easily worked up about →

things that don't matter while neglecting the things that ~~matter~~ matter most?

★ Does the potential fool ignore problems that will create certain ~~doom~~ doom for the business and for their life while neglecting the most important action items ~~they need~~ to take in their life?

Over the years my belief and hope in most of humanity has greatly diminished. For years a member of my extended family has argued that the ~~&~~ AMERICAN health care system is screwed up and that Universal Healthcare is the way to go. Yet when ~~a~~ I show her clearly and ~~specifically~~ specifically why FRANCE, SPAIN, ~~and~~ Canada and other COUNTRIES THAT HAVE Become Socialist in their ~~more~~ worldview are financially struggling she simply argues that greedy capitalism is to blame.

When you find yourself talking with someone who sincerely does not value logic, common sense, rationality or capitalism, run for the hills.

+ Also when you meet a passionate Bernie Sanders fan it's time to run for hills.

> "A positive attitude causes a chain reaction of positive thoughts, events, and outcomes. It is a catalyst that sparks extraordinary results."

- Wade Boggs (Major league baseball hall of fame member)

Chapter 9

Only Listen to G.O.A.T.S. and Invest in Moats

"The fastest way to change yourself is to hang out with people who are already the way you want to be." - Reid Hoffman (The co-founder of Linkedin, a venture capital partner at Greylock Partners, and one of the original partners at PayPal)

As you seek to improve ~~the ap~~ the quality of your life and your family's life it will become increasingly important that you only listen to people who have actually ~~Ach.~~ ~~Acc~~ achieved massive success. In today's culture everybody is a social media expert and a search engine expert if they own a laptop.

In this world of endless distractions it is important that you only listen to organizations and people with a proven track record. It ~~also~~ is also important ~~that~~ you invest into creating the rules and systems needed to prevent yourself from ~~being~~ being reachable ~~from~~ by random solicitors, scammers and time-wasting individuals who want to "just pick your brain."

> "You either pay now or pay later with just about every decision you make about where and how you spend your time."

— Lee Cockerell (Former executive vice president of Walt Disney World Resorts who once managed over 40,000 employees and 1 milllion guests per week)

CHAPTER 10

Avoid People Who Obsess About Arguing About Politics and Religion

"You are the average of the five people you most associate with."
- Tim Ferriss (Best-Selling author, entrepreneur, and podcast host.)

This chapter will be short like the ~~one~~ conversations that you should be having with the members of your team about religion and politics. In a nutshell there are over 33,000 ~~christians~~ christian denominations. ~~This means~~ ~~~~ ~~~~ That people who invest and have invested their entire lives to studying

the Bible and their CHRISTIAN FAITH HAVE DISAGREED WITH EACH OTHER TO THE POINT THAT they have gone on to START THEIR OWN DENOMINATION 33,830 times. DON'T Allow Religious oR politically ~~divisive~~ divisize ~~people to~~ people to hog your meetings ~~and~~ and to waste your time.

> "The only way to get the best of an argument is to avoid it."

- Dale Carnegie (Best-Selling author of *How to Win Friends and Influence People*)

CHAPTER 11

Develop an Action Bias and Avoid Excuse-Making Bureaucrats

GOING & GOING & GOING

"Success seems to be connected with action. Successful men keep moving. They make mistakes, but they keep moving." - Conrad Hilton (Founder of Hilton Hotels)

In order to become successful, you must create an action bias within your organization like Conrad Hilton did when starting the Hilton Hotel chain. If you want to achieve massive success, you simply cannot allow ~~xxxx~~ excuse making ~~bureaucrats~~ bureaucrats to enter your organization or your life.

CHAPTER 12

Burn Bridges to Create Distance

"So, because you are lukewarm--neither hot nor cold--I am about to spit you out of my mouth." - Revelation 3:16

~~There~~ Unfortunately, we all have had perpetually negative ~~people~~ people in our lives at one point or another. However, in order to free yourself from these negative ~~people~~ you people must burn some bridges. You must call some people up and let them know that they are out of your life for good because of the actions they continue to take on a daily basis.

CHAPTER 13

Friends of Your Enemies Are Your Enemies

"Then one of the Twelve--the one called Judas Iscariot--went to the chief priests and asked, "What are you willing to give me if I deliver him over to you?" So they counted out for him thirty pieces of silver." - Matthew 26:15

In your life, whenever you make an enemy, you must ar understand that everyone who is a friend of your enemy is also your enemy. Over the years many employees have left my companies to start businesses to directly compete with me and guess what? Nearly everytime their friends and ex-coworkers →

went on to screw me too. Friends of your enemies are your enemies and once you go out on a limb and stand up for something get ready because you will create enemies.

"You have enemies? Good. That means you've stood up for something sometime in your life." —Winston Churchill (The Prime Minister who stood up to Nazi facism before he had secured American support

In ~~the~~ order for you to live a peaceful and drama free life you must know who your friends and enemies are. Remember the friends of your enemies are your enemies. Who are the friends of your enemies?

Person #1 _____

Person #2 _____

Person #3 _____

Person #4 _____

Person #5 _____

Person #6 _____

NOTE:
You must really be doing something right if you have more than ~~seven~~ SIX people who are friends of your enemies.

PERSON #7 _____
PERSON #8 _____
PERSON #9 _____
PERSON #10 _____
PERSON #11 _____
PERSON #12 _____
PERSON #13 _____
PERSON #14 _____
PERSON #15 _____
PERSON #16 _____

"People around you, constantly under the pull of their emotions, change their ideas by the day or by the hour, depending on their mood. You must never assume that what people say or do in a particular moment is a statement of their permanent desires."

- Robert Greene (Best-Selling author of Mastery)

CHAPTER 14

Don't Compromise Only Spend Time with the Wise

"Without counsel plans fail, but with many advisers they succeed." - Proverbs 15:22

As you climb higher and higher up the mountain of success you will discover there will be less and less people still climbing. In fact, as you hike and climb your way to the top, you will find many people begging for you to stop and help them. However, if you stop and help everyone you too will never reach your goal and the mountain top.

However, once you do reach the top you will want to bring people with you that don't deserve to be up there with you. Don't do it.

Do not compromise. Only spend time with the wise and those who were willing to put in the work to get to the mountain top. When you introduce the whiners to the winners it never goes well.

"Anytime ordinary comes in contact with extraordinary there is a conflict."

- TD Jakes (Best-Selling Author, Pastor, and Media Mogul)

CHAPTER 15

Only Invite Happy "Glampers" (Glamping = Glamorous Camping)

"Surround yourself with great people."
- Lee Cockerell (Former executive vice president of Walt Disney World Resorts who once managed over 40,000 employees and 1 milllion guests per week)

Once ~~[scratched]~~ that moment happens and you realize that you too have become an overnight success story as a result of diligently grinding for 15 years in a row, don't feel guilty about ~~camping~~ camping or "glamping" while living it up. If you want to enjoy "glamorous camping" you should do it. You deserve it.

At this point you have made the trade-offs that were necessary to achieve your goals and you should not feel obligated to invite everyone to figuratively go "glamping" or "camping" with you. Your friends should be only people who you share values and time with, not just people who you geographically lived near or went →

to school with at some point. Keep your "INNER-CIRCLE" tight AND DON'T CONFUSE ~~ACQU ACQUAINTENCE~~ ACQUAINTANCES AS BEING FRIENDS. REMEMBER

"THE SECRET OF HAPPINESS IS MINIMIZING THE AMOUNT OF TIME YOU SPEND WITH people you don't choose to be with."
— PHIL LIBIN
(The former CEO of EVERNOTE)

HERE'S TO YOUR SUCCESS!

PROVERBS 10:4

— Boom!

CLARK
2019

www.ingramcontent.com/pod-product-compliance
Lightning Source LLC
Chambersburg PA
CBHW070439010526
44118CB00014B/2108